Airdrop
Investing 101
How to Make Money While You Sleep…

Henry Otasowere

Airdrop Investing 101

©Copyright 2023 Henry Otasowere, "Airdrop Investing 101: How to Make Money While You Sleep"

ALL RIGHTS RESERVED

No part of this publication may be reproduced, stored in a retrieval system, or transmitted, in any form or by any means, electronic, mechanical, photocopying, recording or otherwise, without the express written permission of the author.

Otimage Publishers

Paper cover - **ISBN:** 9798385744459

CONTENTS

Foreword vi

Acknowledgments ix

Introduction 11

    Chapter 1 13

    What Are Airdrops and Why Invest in Them? 13

    Chapter 2 24

    The Basics of Airdrop Investing: Getting Started 24

Understanding Cryptocurrencies and Tokens 27

Setting Up Your Wallets and Exchanges 30

    Chapter 3 33

    How to Research Airdrops: Finding the Gems 33

Analyzing Whitepapers and Roadmaps 36

Evaluating the Team and Community 39

Scouting for Early Signals and Opportunities 42

    Chapter 4 45

    Building a Diversified Portfolio: Spreading Your Risks 45

Choosing Different Categories and Types of Airdrops 50

Staking airdrops 52

Niche vs. mainstream projects 55

Balancing Your Exposure and Allocations 60

Rebalancing and Adjusting Your Strategy Over Time 63

    Chapter 5 66

    Managing Risk and Avoiding Scams: Staying Safe and Secure 66

Identifying Red Flags and Warning Signs 69

Protecting Your Private Keys and Passwords 72

Learning from Past Mistakes and Lessons 75

    Chapter 6 79

    Advanced Strategies and Tools: Maximizing Your Returns 79

Arbitrage	84
Technical analysis	90
Leveraging Staking, Yield Farming, and Liquidity Mining	97
Using Analytics, Trading Bots, and Signals	101
Collaborating with Communities and Networks	110
Chapter 7	115
Conclusion: Airdrop Investing as a Sustainable and Profitable Venture.	115

Foreword

Investing can be a daunting task, but it is also an essential part of building wealth and achieving financial freedom. With so many investment options available today, it can be challenging to find the right strategy that fits your goals, preferences, and risk tolerance.

One investment opportunity that has emerged in recent years is airdrops. Airdrops are a form of cryptocurrency distribution in which tokens are given away for free or in exchange for a small action, such as following a social media account or completing a survey.

Airdrops can be an excellent source of passive income, as they can appreciate in value over time or provide access to exclusive benefits and features.

However, investing in airdrops requires a certain level of knowledge and skills, as well as careful research and management.

That's where this book comes in. "Airdrop Investing 101: How to Make Money While You Sleep" is a comprehensive guide that teaches readers how to invest in airdrops and maximize their returns.

The book covers all aspects of airdrop investing, from the basics of cryptocurrencies and wallets to advanced strategies and tools.

It provides practical tips and insights on how to research airdrops, build a diversified portfolio, manage risks, and avoid scams.

It also offers real-world examples and case studies of successful airdrop investors and their journeys.

What sets this book apart is its practical and reader-friendly approach. The author, a seasoned investor and educator, has distilled his knowledge and experience into a concise and accessible guide that anyone can follow.

The book is written in a clear and engaging style, with helpful illustrations and examples.

Whether you are a seasoned investor looking for new opportunities or a beginner who wants to start investing in airdrops, this book is for you.

It will equip you with the skills and confidence to navigate the world of airdrop investing and make money while you sleep.

I highly recommend "Airdrop Investing 101: How to Make Money While You Sleep" to anyone who wants to take their financial future into their own hands and invest in a promising and exciting market.

John Smith

Investment Advisor and Author of "The Smart Investor's Handbook"

Acknowledgments

Writing a book is never a solo effort. It takes a team of dedicated and talented individuals to bring an idea to life and turn it into a tangible product. I am grateful to everyone who has contributed to the making of "Airdrop Investing 101: How to Make Money While You Sleep."

First and foremost, I would like to thank my spiritual father, Joshua Iginla, who has been instrumental in shaping and refining me to the man I become. I am also grateful to the production team at Otimage Publishers, who have worked tirelessly to design, format, and distribute the book.

I would like to express my gratitude to the cryptocurrency community, which has inspired and motivated me to write this book. Without the support and enthusiasm of fellow investors, traders, and developers, this book would not have been possible. I also want to thank the founders and teams of the various projects and platforms mentioned in the book, who have created innovative and valuable products that benefit investors and users alike.

I would like to acknowledge my friends and family, who have been a constant source of encouragement and inspiration throughout my writing journey. Their support and understanding have helped me to overcome challenges and stay focused on my goals. I am especially grateful to my partner, my wife,

(Andreia Otasowere) who has been my biggest cheerleader and critique, and who has provided invaluable feedback and insights.

Last but not least, I would like to thank the readers of this book, who have shown an interest in airdrop investing and who have entrusted me with their time and attention. I hope that this book will provide you with practical knowledge and insights that will help you to achieve your investment goals and to build a better financial future.

Thank you all for being a part of this project and for making it a reality.

Sincerely,

Henry Otasowere

Introduction

Welcome to "Airdrop Investing 101: How to Make Money While You Sleep." This book is designed to be a comprehensive guide for anyone who wants to invest in airdrops and benefit from the booming cryptocurrency market. Airdrops are a form of cryptocurrency distribution in which tokens are given away for free or in exchange for a small action, such as following a social media account or completing a survey. Airdrops can be an excellent source of passive income, as they can appreciate in value over time or provide access to exclusive benefits and features.

Investing in airdrops can be an exciting and profitable venture, but it also requires a certain level of knowledge and skills. You need to know how to research airdrops, build a diversified portfolio, manage risks, and avoid scams. You also need to be aware of the latest trends and developments in the cryptocurrency market and be able to adapt to changing conditions.

That's where this book comes in. "Airdrop Investing 101" provides a step-by-step guide to investing in airdrops and maximizing your returns. The book covers all aspects of airdrop investing, from the basics of cryptocurrencies and wallets to advanced strategies and tools. It provides practical tips and insights on how to research airdrops, build a diversified portfolio, manage risks, and avoid scams.

It also offers real-world examples and case studies of successful airdrop investors and their journeys.

This book is divided into seven chapters. Chapter One provides an introduction to airdrops and their potential benefits. Chapter Two covers the basics of cryptocurrencies and wallets, which are essential for airdrop investing. Chapter Three explains how to research airdrops and find the best opportunities. Chapter Four teaches you how to build a diversified portfolio and manage your risks. Chapter Five focuses on how to stay safe and secure while investing in airdrops and avoid scams. Chapter Six covers advanced strategies and tools that can help you maximize your returns. Finally, Chapter Seven provides a conclusion and a summary of the main points covered in the book.

This book is written for anyone who wants to learn about airdrop investing, regardless of their level of experience or expertise. Whether you are a seasoned investor looking for new opportunities or a beginner who wants to start investing in airdrops, this book is for you. It will equip you with the skills and confidence to navigate the world of airdrop investing and make money while you sleep.

So, let's get started on this exciting journey together.

CHAPTER 1

WHAT ARE AIRDROPS AND WHY INVEST IN THEM?

Cryptocurrencies have been a hot topic for years, with Bitcoin and other digital currencies dominating headlines and sparking curiosity in investors around the world. However, airdrops are a lesser-known opportunity in the cryptocurrency space that can offer a significant return on investment.

An airdrop is a marketing strategy used by cryptocurrency projects to distribute their tokens to a larger audience. In a typical airdrop, tokens are given away for free or in exchange for a small action, such as following a social media account or completing a survey. This enables cryptocurrency projects to reach a wider audience and build a community around their product.

So, why invest in airdrops? Here are some of the main reasons:

Potential for high returns

Airdrops can provide a significant return on investment, especially if the tokens distributed appreciate in value over time. Some airdrops have seen gains of over 1000%, providing a potentially lucrative investment opportunity.

Airdrops have the potential to provide investors with high returns, making them an attractive investment opportunity. The potential for high returns comes from the fact that airdropped tokens are usually distributed at a very early stage in a cryptocurrency project's lifecycle, often before the project has launched or even before its whitepaper has been released.

If the cryptocurrency project is successful, and the tokens appreciate in value over time, the initial airdrop can turn into a significant investment opportunity. For example, if an investor receives 100 tokens as part of an airdrop, and those tokens appreciate in value by 1000%, the investor's initial investment of zero could be worth a substantial amount of money.

It is important to note, however, that the potential for high returns also comes with a significant risk of loss. Not all cryptocurrency projects are successful, and many projects fail to gain traction in the market. Additionally, the value of cryptocurrency tokens can be highly volatile, with significant fluctuations in price over short periods of time. Investors should be aware of the risks involved in airdrop investing and should only invest what they can afford to lose.

To maximize the potential for high returns, investors should carefully research the cryptocurrency project before participating in an airdrop. This includes reading the project's whitepaper, examining the project's team and advisors, and analyzing the project's market potential. It is also important to diversify your portfolio by investing in multiple cryptocurrency projects to spread your risk.

Airdrops have the potential to provide investors with high returns, but they also come with significant risk. Investors should carefully research each project and analyze its potential for success before investing in an airdrop.

By doing so, investors can potentially reap the rewards of a successful cryptocurrency project and turn their initial airdrop investment into a significant return.

Access to exclusive benefits and features

Some airdrops are designed to provide access to exclusive benefits and features of a cryptocurrency project. This can include early access to a new product or service, discounts on fees, or access to unique functionalities.

In addition to the potential for high returns, another benefit of participating in airdrops is access to exclusive benefits and features. Some cryptocurrency projects use airdrops as a way to incentivize early adopters and provide them with exclusive access to certain features or benefits.

For example, a cryptocurrency project may offer an airdrop to users who hold a certain amount of tokens, granting them early access to a new product or service before it is made available to the general public.

This can give early adopters a significant advantage over other users and provide them with a unique opportunity to experience the benefits of a new product or service before anyone else.

Additionally, some airdrops may provide users with discounts on transaction fees or access to unique functionalities that are not available to the general public. These benefits can provide significant value to users, making participation in the airdrop even more attractive.

It is important to note that not all airdrops offer exclusive benefits or features. Some airdrops simply distribute tokens to a large number of participants without any additional benefits.

Investors should carefully research each airdrop before participating to determine whether it offers any exclusive benefits or features.

Airdrops can provide investors with access to exclusive benefits and features of a cryptocurrency project, giving them a unique advantage over other users. Investors should carefully research each airdrop to determine whether it offers any exclusive benefits or features and weigh the potential benefits against the risks before investing.

Diversification

Investing in airdrops can help diversify your investment portfolio, as they offer exposure to a range of different cryptocurrency projects and products. This can help mitigate risk and provide a more balanced investment strategy.

Investing in airdrops can also help diversify an investor's portfolio, as it offers exposure to a range of different cryptocurrency projects and products. By investing in multiple airdrops, an investor can spread their risk across different projects, mitigating the risk of any one project failing.

Diversification is an essential component of any investment strategy, as it helps to balance risk and potential reward. By investing in a range of different cryptocurrency projects, an investor can potentially benefit from the success of multiple projects, even if one or more projects fail.

Airdrops offer a unique opportunity for diversification, as they often provide access to a range of different cryptocurrency projects and products that may not be available through traditional investment channels. For example, an airdrop may provide access to a new decentralized finance (DeFi) platform or a new blockchain-based gaming project.

Investing in airdrops can also provide exposure to emerging technologies and trends in the cryptocurrency space. This can be particularly beneficial for investors who are looking to invest in the future of blockchain technology and cryptocurrency.

Investing in airdrops can help diversify an investor's portfolio, providing exposure to a range of different cryptocurrency projects and products. This can help mitigate risk and provide a more balanced investment strategy. However, as with any investment, it is important to carefully research each airdrop and weigh the potential benefits against the risks before investing.

Low entry barrier

Airdrops typically have a low barrier to entry, as they often require minimal effort or investment on the part of the investor. This makes them an accessible investment opportunity for anyone, regardless of their level of experience or expertise.

Another advantage of investing in airdrops is that they typically have a low barrier to entry. Unlike many traditional investment opportunities that require significant capital or expertise, airdrops often require minimal effort or investment on the part of the investor.

For example, some airdrops may simply require users to sign up for a project's email list or follow their social media accounts to receive tokens. Others may require users to complete simple tasks, such as filling out a survey or sharing a project on social media.

This low barrier to entry makes airdrops an accessible investment opportunity for anyone, regardless of their level of experience or expertise. Even investors with limited funds or knowledge of the cryptocurrency market can potentially benefit from participating in airdrops.

Additionally, airdrops can provide an opportunity for investors to test the waters and gain experience with investing in cryptocurrency projects without committing significant capital. By participating in multiple airdrops, investors can gain exposure to a range of different projects and products and learn more about the cryptocurrency market and investing strategies.

However, it is important to note that the low barrier to entry also means that airdrops can be highly competitive, with a large number of users vying for a limited number of tokens. Investors should carefully research each airdrop and weigh the potential benefits against the risks before investing.

The low barrier to entry of airdrops makes them an accessible investment opportunity for anyone, regardless of their level of experience or expertise. This can provide investors with an opportunity to gain experience with investing in cryptocurrency projects and potentially benefit from the success of multiple projects.

Opportunity for community building

Airdrops can be an opportunity to engage with a community of like-minded individuals who share a common interest in a cryptocurrency project. This can be a valuable resource for learning and staying up-to-date with the latest developments in the cryptocurrency market.

In addition to the potential financial benefits, investing in airdrops can also provide an opportunity for community building. Airdrops often attract a community of investors who are interested in the same cryptocurrency project or product, creating a space for discussion, collaboration, and learning.

By participating in an airdrop, investors can join a community of like-minded individuals who share a common interest in the project. This can provide a valuable resource for learning about the project and staying up-to-date with the latest developments in the cryptocurrency market.

Community building can also create opportunities for collaboration and networking. Investors may be able to connect with other investors or even members of the project's development team, which can provide valuable insights and opportunities for further investment or involvement in the project.

Furthermore, by participating in airdrops, investors may have the opportunity to provide feedback or contribute to the development of the project. Some projects may even offer rewards or incentives for community members who provide valuable feedback or contribute to the project's development.

Investing in airdrops can provide an opportunity for community building and engagement with like-minded individuals who share a common interest in a cryptocurrency project or product. This can be a valuable resource for learning about the project, staying up-to-date with the latest developments in the cryptocurrency market, and creating opportunities for collaboration and networking.

Airdrops offer a unique investment opportunity that can provide a range of benefits, including high returns, access to exclusive benefits, diversification, a low entry barrier, and community building. In the next chapter, we will cover the basics of cryptocurrencies and wallets, which are essential for airdrop investing.

In this chapter, we will explore the different types of airdrops and how they work. There are several types of airdrops, including:

Standard Airdrops:

This is the most common type of airdrop, where tokens are given away for free to a large number of people. Participants are typically required to perform a small action, such as following a social media account, to be eligible for the airdrop.

Holder Airdrops: This type of airdrop is targeted at existing token holders of a cryptocurrency project. It is designed to reward loyal token holders and encourage them to hold onto their tokens for a longer period of time.

Fork Airdrops: A fork airdrop occurs when a new cryptocurrency project is created as a result of a fork in an existing blockchain. Existing token holders of the original blockchain are given the equivalent number of tokens in the new project.

Bounty Airdrops: Bounty airdrops are a type of airdrop where participants are rewarded for completing specific tasks, such as bug reporting or content creation. This type of airdrop is designed to encourage community participation and engagement.

Exclusive Airdrops: Exclusive airdrops are typically offered to a select group of people, such as investors or influencers. These airdrops can provide access to exclusive benefits or opportunities that are not available to the general public.

Each type of airdrop has its own unique characteristics and benefits, and understanding the differences between them is crucial for successful airdrop investing.

In addition to understanding the different types of airdrops, it is also important to be aware of the risks involved in airdrop investing. While airdrops can provide high returns, they also carry a significant risk of scams and fraud. In the next chapter, we will explore the basics of cryptocurrencies and wallets, which are essential for airdrop investing and mitigating risk.

CHAPTER 2
THE BASICS OF AIRDROP INVESTING: GETTING STARTED

When it comes to getting started with airdrop investing, there are some key basics that many investors may not be aware of. One of the most important things to keep in mind is that not all airdrops are created equal, and investors need to carefully evaluate each opportunity before investing.

Firstly, it's important to research the project behind the airdrop and understand its goals, team, and track record. Investors should look for projects that have a strong team with relevant experience and a track record of delivering on their promises.

Secondly, it's important to evaluate the token being distributed in the airdrop. Some tokens may have a limited use case or be issued solely for speculative purposes, while others may have a clear utility and use case within the project ecosystem.

Investors should also consider the distribution mechanism of the airdrop. Some airdrops may distribute tokens on a first-come, first-served basis, while others may use a lottery system or other mechanism to distribute tokens fairly. Investors should evaluate the distribution mechanism and assess the likelihood of receiving a significant number of tokens.

Another important aspect of airdrop investing is managing risk. While airdrops can be a lucrative investment opportunity, they can also be highly speculative and involve significant risk. Investors should carefully evaluate the potential risks and rewards of each airdrop opportunity and diversify their investment portfolio to mitigate risk.

Finally, investors should be aware of the tax implications of airdrop investing. In some cases, airdrops may be considered taxable income and subject to capital gains tax. It's important to consult with a tax professional to understand the tax implications of airdrop investing and ensure compliance with tax laws.

In conclusion, getting started with airdrop investing requires careful evaluation of each opportunity and an understanding of the potential risks and rewards. By researching the project behind the airdrop, evaluating the token being distributed, managing risk, and understanding tax implications, investors can make informed investment decisions and potentially benefit from this exciting investment opportunity.

Additionally, it's important to be mindful of scams in the airdrop space. Airdrop scams have become increasingly common, with fraudsters impersonating legitimate projects and tricking investors into giving away personal information or sending funds in exchange for promised airdrops that never materialize. Investors should be wary of airdrops that require them to send funds or provide personal information, and should always verify the legitimacy of the project and airdrop before participating.

Investors should also be aware of the technical requirements for participating in airdrops. Some airdrops may require investors to use specific wallets or participate in certain blockchain networks, and it's important to have a basic understanding of these technical requirements before investing.

Furthermore, it's worth noting that airdrop investing is a dynamic and evolving space, with new projects and opportunities emerging regularly. Investors should stay up-to-date with the latest news and developments in the airdrop space to ensure they are making informed investment decisions.

It's important to have realistic expectations when it comes to airdrop investing. While airdrops can provide a significant return on investment, they are not a guaranteed way to make money and involve significant risk.

Investors should approach airdrop investing as they would any other investment opportunity, with a clear understanding of the risks and rewards involved. With proper research and risk management, airdrop investing can be a valuable addition to a diversified investment portfolio.

Understanding Cryptocurrencies and Tokens

One thing that many people may not know about cryptocurrencies and tokens is the difference between the two. While both are digital assets, cryptocurrencies are designed to be used as a medium of exchange, similar to traditional fiat currencies like the US dollar or Euro. Examples of cryptocurrencies include Bitcoin, Ethereum, and Litecoin.

On the other hand, tokens are digital assets that are created and managed on top of a blockchain network, typically using a smart contract. Tokens can represent a wide range of assets, including utility tokens, security tokens, and asset-backed tokens. Examples of tokens include ERC-20 tokens on the Ethereum network and BEP-20 tokens on the Binance Smart Chain.

Another important concept to understand is the role of blockchain technology in the cryptocurrency and token space. Blockchains are decentralized, distributed ledger technologies that allow for secure and transparent record-keeping.

Cryptocurrencies and tokens are typically built on top of a blockchain network, which provides a secure and transparent way to store and transfer digital assets.

It's also important to note that the value of cryptocurrencies and tokens is highly volatile and subject to significant fluctuations. The value of these assets is largely driven by market demand and can be impacted by a wide range of factors, including regulatory changes, market sentiment, and technological advancements.

It's worth noting that the cryptocurrency and token space is constantly evolving, with new projects and technologies emerging regularly. Investors should stay up-to-date with the latest news and developments in the space to ensure they are making informed investment decisions. Additionally, investors should approach cryptocurrencies and tokens with caution and always conduct thorough research before investing, as these assets involve significant risk.

Another important aspect to understand about cryptocurrencies and tokens is the difference between centralized and decentralized networks. Centralized networks are managed by a single entity or organization, which controls the network's operations and makes decisions about the network's development and governance.

In contrast, decentralized networks are managed by a community of participants, with no central authority or organization controlling the network.

Many cryptocurrencies and tokens are built on top of decentralized networks, which offer a range of potential benefits, including greater transparency, increased security, and improved privacy. However, decentralized networks also pose unique challenges, such as the need for community consensus on network upgrades and the potential for governance disputes.

Another key concept to understand is the role of wallets in managing cryptocurrencies and tokens. A wallet is a software program or device that stores private keys, which are used to access and manage digital assets on a blockchain network.

There are many different types of wallets available, including hardware wallets, software wallets, and web wallets. It's important for investors to choose a wallet that meets their specific needs and offers robust security features to protect their assets.

It's worth noting that the regulatory landscape around cryptocurrencies and tokens is still evolving, with many countries implementing new rules and guidelines around the use and trading of digital assets.

Investors should be aware of the regulatory environment in their country or region and ensure they are complying with all applicable laws and regulations.

Setting Up Your Wallets and Exchanges

When setting up wallets and exchanges for cryptocurrency investing, there are a few key things to keep in mind that many people may not be aware of.

First, it's important to choose a reputable wallet or exchange that offers strong security features to protect your assets. Look for wallets or exchanges that offer two-factor authentication, secure login protocols, and other security measures to keep your funds safe.

Second, it's important to understand the fees associated with using wallets and exchanges. Many wallets and exchanges charge fees for transactions or withdrawals, and these fees can vary widely depending on the platform you're using. Be sure to research the fees associated with each wallet or exchange you're considering to ensure that you're getting the best deal.

Third, it's important to understand the different types of wallets and exchanges available. There are hardware wallets, software wallets, and web wallets, each with their own unique advantages and disadvantages. Similarly, there are centralized exchanges, decentralized exchanges, and peer-to-peer marketplaces, each with their own unique features and risks. Be sure to research each option thoroughly and choose the wallet or exchange that best meets your needs.

Fourth, it's important to understand the tax implications of using wallets and exchanges for cryptocurrency investing. In many countries, cryptocurrency transactions are subject to capital gains taxes or other taxes, and it's important to understand your obligations and ensure that you're reporting your transactions correctly.

It's important to keep your wallets and exchanges up-to-date and secure. This means regularly updating your software, using strong passwords, and taking other security precautions to prevent unauthorized access to your funds. With the right precautions and knowledge, setting up wallets and exchanges for cryptocurrency investing can be a straightforward and rewarding process.

In addition to the above points, there are some other things to consider when setting up your wallets and exchanges for cryptocurrency investing.

One important consideration is the level of customer support offered by the wallet or exchange. In the event that you encounter issues with your account or transactions, it's important to have access to prompt and helpful customer support. Look for wallets and exchanges that offer multiple channels of support, such as email, phone, or live chat, and check online reviews to gauge the quality of their customer service.

Another consideration is the regulatory environment in which the wallet or exchange operates. Different countries have different regulations around cryptocurrency, and some wallets and exchanges may not be available in certain regions. Be sure to check whether the wallet or exchange is compliant with local regulations and whether it's available in your country before signing up.

It's also important to understand the risks associated with storing your cryptocurrency on a wallet or exchange. While many wallets and exchanges have strong security features, they are still vulnerable to hacking or other security breaches. Consider diversifying your holdings across multiple wallets and exchanges to reduce the risk of losing all your funds in the event of a security breach.

Be sure to research the reputation and history of the wallet or exchange you're considering. Look for platforms that have been operating for several years and have a strong track record of security and customer support. Check online forums and reviews to get a sense of the experiences of other users, and be wary of any platforms that have a history of security breaches or other issues.

Chapter **3**
HOW TO RESEARCH AIRDROPS: FINDING THE GEMS

When it comes to researching airdrops, there are several factors to consider that can help you identify the best opportunities and avoid scams or low-quality projects.

One key factor is the credibility and reputation of the cryptocurrency project offering the airdrop. Look for projects that have a strong team with relevant experience in the industry, a clear roadmap for development and growth, and a history of delivering on their promises.

Another important consideration is the potential for the token to appreciate in value over time. Look for projects that have a clear use case for their token and a strong demand for their product or service. You may also want to research the market cap and trading volume of the token to get a sense of its liquidity and potential for growth.

It's also important to read the terms and conditions of the airdrop carefully to understand the requirements for participation and any potential restrictions or limitations. Some airdrops may require you to hold a certain amount of a particular cryptocurrency or to complete certain tasks, such as following the project on social media or referring new users.

When researching airdrops, it's also important to be wary of scams and fraudulent projects. Look for red flags such as promises of unrealistic returns, lack of transparency or information about the project, or requests for personal information or cryptocurrency payments.

In addition to these factors, it can also be helpful to join online communities and forums related to cryptocurrency investing to stay up-to-date with the latest news and trends in the industry. This can help you identify new opportunities for airdrops and connect with other investors who can offer insights and advice.

One lesser-known aspect of researching airdrops is the potential for collaboration and partnerships between different cryptocurrency projects. By keeping an eye on news and announcements from various projects, you may be able to identify opportunities for airdrops that are associated with collaborative efforts or partnerships.

For example, if you notice that two or more projects have announced a partnership or collaboration, there may be an opportunity for an airdrop that rewards users who hold both tokens. Similarly, if a project is planning to integrate with a popular cryptocurrency wallet or exchange, there may be an airdrop associated with this integration that rewards users who participate.

Another key aspect of researching airdrops is understanding the different types of airdrops that are available. In addition to traditional airdrops that distribute tokens to a wide audience, there are also targeted airdrops that are designed to reward specific groups or individuals, such as early investors or active community members.

Targeted airdrops can be a valuable opportunity for investors who are already involved in a particular cryptocurrency project or community, as they can provide additional rewards for their involvement and dedication.

Ultimately, the key to successful airdrop investing is to stay informed, do your research, and be mindful of potential risks and scams. By following these guidelines and staying up-to-date with the latest trends and developments in the cryptocurrency market, you can identify the best opportunities for airdrop investing and maximize your potential returns.

Analyzing Whitepapers and Roadmaps

Whitepapers and roadmaps are two essential documents that can provide investors with valuable insights into a cryptocurrency project's technology, business model, and future plans. However, many people may not know how to analyze these documents effectively.

One important thing to keep in mind when analyzing whitepapers and roadmaps is to look beyond the marketing hype and focus on the project's actual technology and use case. Many projects may have flashy marketing materials but lack a clear value proposition or viable product. Therefore, it's essential to read the whitepaper thoroughly and evaluate the project's technical specifications, underlying technology, and potential real-world applications.

Another important consideration is the team behind the project. A strong and experienced team with a proven track record can be a positive sign for investors, as it indicates that the project is well-equipped to execute on its plans and deliver on its promises.

In addition to evaluating the project's technology and team, it's also essential to pay attention to the project's roadmap. A roadmap outlines the project's planned milestones, releases, and development progress over time. By analyzing the roadmap, investors can gain insight into the project's short and long-term goals, as well as its overall progress towards achieving these goals.

However, it's important to remember that a roadmap is not a guarantee of future success or progress. The cryptocurrency market is highly volatile, and unexpected challenges and setbacks can arise at any time. Therefore, investors should approach any investment opportunity with caution and always be prepared for potential risks and uncertainties.

Analyzing whitepapers and roadmaps is a critical component of effective airdrop investing. By evaluating a project's underlying technology, team, and roadmap, investors can make more informed investment decisions and increase their chances of success in the highly competitive cryptocurrency market.

When analyzing whitepapers, it's also important to pay attention to the project's token economics. Token economics refers to the design and distribution of a cryptocurrency's tokens, including its total supply, circulation, and the incentives and rewards offered to users and investors.

Investors should look for projects that have a well-designed and sustainable token economics model. This means that the token supply and distribution should be carefully planned to ensure that there is a healthy balance between supply and demand. Additionally, the incentives and rewards offered to users and investors should be designed to encourage participation and growth, without artificially inflating the value of the token.

Another important factor to consider when analyzing whitepapers is the project's legal and regulatory compliance. Cryptocurrency projects operate in a highly regulated environment, and it's essential to ensure that the project is compliant with relevant laws and regulations. Failure to comply with these regulations can result in legal and financial consequences for the project and its investors.

When it comes to analyzing roadmaps, investors should look for projects that have a clear and realistic plan for development and growth. A well-designed roadmap should outline the project's key milestones and progress towards achieving its goals, as well as the challenges and risks that may arise along the way.

However, it's important to keep in mind that a roadmap is not set in stone and may change over time. Investors should be prepared for unexpected delays, setbacks, or changes in direction, and should always keep an eye on the project's progress and development.

Analyzing whitepapers and roadmaps is a complex but critical part of airdrop investing. By evaluating a project's technology, team, token economics, and regulatory compliance, as well as its roadmap and progress, investors can make more informed investment decisions and increase their chances of success in the highly competitive and rapidly evolving cryptocurrency market.

Evaluating the Team and Community

When evaluating a cryptocurrency project, it's important to take a close look at the team behind the project and the community of users and supporters that it has attracted. While a project's technology and token economics are certainly important, the people behind the project are often just as critical to its success.

One thing that many people may not know about when evaluating the team is the importance of diversity. A diverse team can bring a wide range of perspectives and experiences to the project, which can help to ensure that the project is designed and developed with a broad range of users and stakeholders in mind. Investors should look for teams that include individuals with diverse backgrounds, skills, and experiences.

It's also important to look for teams that have a track record of success and experience in relevant fields. For example, a team with experience in blockchain development, software engineering, or finance may be better equipped to handle the technical and financial challenges of a cryptocurrency project.

In addition to evaluating the team, investors should also look closely at the project's community of users and supporters. A strong and engaged community can be a powerful force behind a cryptocurrency project, helping to drive adoption, user engagement, and growth.

Investors should look for projects that have an active and supportive community of users and supporters, as well as a clear plan for community building and engagement. This may include regular updates and communication with the community, incentives and rewards for user participation, and opportunities for users to contribute to the project's development and growth.

Finally, it's important to keep in mind that evaluating the team and community is an ongoing process. Investors should stay up-to-date with the latest developments and changes within the project and its community, and be prepared to adjust their investment strategy as needed based on new information and insights.

Another important factor to consider when evaluating the team and community is the level of transparency and accountability that they demonstrate. Investors should look for teams that are open and honest about their goals, strategies, and progress, and who are willing to engage with their community and address any concerns or questions that arise.

One way to gauge the level of transparency and accountability within a project is to look at its governance model. A project with a clear and well-defined governance model can help to ensure that decision-making is transparent, fair, and inclusive. Investors should look for projects that have clear guidelines and processes for decision-making, as well as mechanisms for feedback and community input.

Another important factor to consider is the level of trust and credibility that the team and project have within the wider cryptocurrency community. This can be influenced by a range of factors, including the team's reputation, past successes or failures, and the project's track record in delivering on its promises and meeting its goals.

Investors should take the time to research the project and team thoroughly, looking for any red flags or warning signs that may indicate potential issues or concerns. This may include investigating past projects or businesses associated with the team, conducting due diligence on the project's technical infrastructure and token economics, and monitoring social media and community forums for any signs of controversy or conflict.

Ultimately, the key to successfully evaluating the team and community of a cryptocurrency project is to approach it with a critical and discerning eye, and to be prepared to adapt and adjust your investment strategy as needed based on new information and insights. By doing so, investors can help to minimize their risk and maximize their potential returns in the exciting and rapidly evolving world of cryptocurrency investing.

Scouting for Early Signals and Opportunities

Scouting for early signals and opportunities is a crucial aspect of airdrop investing, and one that many investors overlook or fail to prioritize. The cryptocurrency market is highly volatile and fast-moving, and new opportunities can arise and disappear quickly. As such, it is important for investors to stay vigilant and alert for early signals and emerging trends in the market.

One effective way to scout for early signals and opportunities is to stay up-to-date with the latest news and developments in the cryptocurrency market. This can involve monitoring social media and community forums, subscribing to industry newsletters and publications, and following key thought leaders and influencers in the space.

Investors should also be on the lookout for emerging trends and technologies within the cryptocurrency market, such as new blockchain protocols, emerging use cases for blockchain technology, and innovative new products and services. By staying ahead of the curve and anticipating future trends and developments, investors can position themselves to capitalize on new opportunities as they arise.

Another important aspect of scouting for early signals and opportunities is to keep a close eye on market sentiment and investor behavior. This can involve monitoring trading volumes, tracking price trends and technical indicators, and analyzing patterns in buying and selling behavior.

By staying attuned to market sentiment and investor behavior, investors can gain valuable insights into the underlying drivers of market movements and make more informed investment decisions. This can be especially important in the highly volatile and unpredictable world of cryptocurrency investing, where market sentiment can shift rapidly and unexpectedly.

Ultimately, scouting for early signals and opportunities is a key aspect of airdrop investing that can help investors to identify and capitalize on emerging trends and opportunities in the market. By staying vigilant and proactive, investors can position themselves to stay ahead of the curve and maximize their potential returns in this exciting and rapidly evolving space.

When scouting for early signals and opportunities, it is important to keep an eye on industry news and developments. This includes monitoring social media channels, forums, and chat groups, as well as attending industry events and conferences.

In addition to industry news, it is also important to pay attention to regulatory changes and updates, as these can have a significant impact on the cryptocurrency market. For example, if a major regulatory agency announces a crackdown on a certain type of cryptocurrency, it could cause a drop in the market value of that cryptocurrency.

Another key aspect to keep in mind when scouting for early signals and opportunities is the importance of timing. Cryptocurrency markets can be highly volatile, and prices can fluctuate rapidly. By keeping a close eye on market trends and analyzing historical data, investors can identify potential entry and exit points for their investments.

Furthermore, it is important to exercise caution when investing in airdrops that offer high returns or seem too good to be true. These may be scams or fraudulent projects, and investors may end up losing their investment. It is essential to conduct thorough due diligence and research before investing in any cryptocurrency project or airdrop.

Chapter **4**

BUILDING A DIVERSIFIED PORTFOLIO: SPREADING YOUR RISKS

When it comes to building a diversified portfolio in airdrop investing, it's important to remember that not all tokens are created equal. While some tokens may have high potential for growth, others may be less promising. It's important to assess the risks and rewards of each token and project before investing.

One aspect that many people may not consider when building a diversified portfolio is the importance of investing in both established and emerging projects. Established projects with a proven track record can provide stability and a sense of security, while emerging projects may offer higher potential returns. By investing in a mix of established and emerging projects, investors can balance risk and reward and improve their chances of success.

Another important factor to consider when building a diversified portfolio is the importance of balancing exposure to different sectors and industries. Cryptocurrency is a rapidly evolving and diverse field, and different sectors may have varying levels of risk and potential reward. For example, investing solely in decentralized finance (DeFi) projects may provide high potential returns but may also be riskier than investing in a mix of DeFi, non-fungible tokens (NFTs), and other sectors.

Investors should also pay attention to the correlation between different tokens in their portfolio. Correlation refers to how closely the price of one token is related to the price of another token. Tokens that are highly correlated may move in sync, while tokens with low correlation may move independently. By investing in tokens with low correlation, investors can diversify their portfolio and reduce overall risk.

Finally, investors should regularly review and rebalance their portfolio to ensure that it remains diversified and aligned with their investment goals. By periodically assessing their portfolio and making adjustments as needed, investors can improve their chances of success in airdrop investing.

One important aspect that many people may not know about when building a diversified portfolio of airdrops is the need to consider the correlation between different tokens. Correlation refers to the degree to which the price movements of two or more tokens are related. Tokens with high correlation tend to move in the same direction, while those with low correlation tend to move independently of each other.

Therefore, it is important to consider the correlation between different tokens when building a diversified portfolio of airdrops. Investing in a portfolio of airdrops that are highly correlated with each other may not provide the desired level of diversification and may increase the overall risk of the portfolio. On the other hand, investing in a portfolio of airdrops that have low correlation with each other may provide a better level of diversification and may help reduce overall portfolio risk.

Another consideration when building a diversified portfolio of airdrops is the need to consider the different stages of the token distribution process. Airdrops may be distributed at different stages of a project's development, such as during the ICO or after the project has launched. A portfolio that includes a mix of tokens at different stages of development may provide a better level of diversification and may reduce the overall risk of the portfolio.

Finally, it is important to consider the overall size and allocation of your portfolio. While diversification can help reduce risk, it is also important to avoid spreading your investments too thin. Investing in too many airdrops or allocating too small of a percentage of your portfolio to each airdrop may not provide the desired level of return and may increase overall portfolio risk.

Another important factor to consider when building a diversified portfolio is to ensure that your investments are not overly correlated. This means that you should avoid investing in airdrops that are related to the same industry or project, as they may be influenced by similar market trends and events.

For instance, if you invest in airdrops related to decentralized finance (DeFi) projects, you may want to diversify your portfolio by including airdrops related to other sectors such as gaming or social media. This can help reduce your exposure to risks associated with any one industry or project.

Additionally, it is important to regularly review and rebalance your portfolio to ensure that it remains diversified and aligned with your investment goals. This can involve selling investments that are underperforming and reallocating your funds to other airdrops that offer better potential returns.

Overall, building a diversified portfolio requires careful research, analysis, and monitoring, but it can help you manage risk and maximize returns in the long run.

Another important aspect to consider when building a diversified portfolio is the size of your investments. It is generally recommended to invest only a small portion of your total investment capital in any single airdrop project, especially if it is a new or untested project.

This can help you manage risk and reduce the potential impact of any losses. For instance, if you allocate 5% of your investment capital to a single airdrop project, you will still have 95% of your funds available to invest in other projects if that particular airdrop does not perform well.

Furthermore, it is also important to consider the liquidity of your investments. This refers to how easily you can convert your investments into cash if needed.

Some airdrops may have low liquidity, meaning that it can be difficult to sell your tokens quickly or at a reasonable price. This can be an important consideration if you may need to access your funds in the short term.

Finally, you may also want to consider using a dollar-cost averaging (DCA) strategy when investing in airdrops. DCA involves investing a fixed amount of money into a particular investment at regular intervals, regardless of the current market conditions.

This can help you avoid the temptation to invest large sums of money during market highs and potentially lose money during market downturns.

Choosing Different Categories and Types of Airdrops

When it comes to choosing different categories and types of airdrops, many people may not be aware of the various options available to them. Airdrops can be categorized in different ways, and each category has its own set of advantages and risks. Here are some categories and types of airdrops to consider:

Platform-specific airdrops: These airdrops are distributed by a specific blockchain platform or cryptocurrency. For example, an airdrop may be offered to holders of a particular cryptocurrency or to those who have completed certain tasks on a specific blockchain platform. Platform-specific airdrops can be a good way to gain exposure to a particular cryptocurrency or blockchain project.

Bounty airdrops: These airdrops are distributed to users who complete specific tasks, such as sharing a project on social media, creating content, or referring friends. Bounty airdrops can be a good way to earn tokens without having to invest money.

Exchange airdrops: Some exchanges offer airdrops to users who hold a certain amount of cryptocurrency on their platform. These airdrops can be a good way to earn tokens while also using a trusted exchange platform.

Fork airdrops: Fork airdrops occur when a cryptocurrency splits into two, and holders of the original cryptocurrency receive a new cryptocurrency as a result. Fork airdrops can be a good way to receive free tokens without having to invest in a new cryptocurrency.

Hard fork airdrops: Similar to fork airdrops, hard fork airdrops occur when a cryptocurrency undergoes a significant change that results in a new cryptocurrency being created. Hard fork airdrops can be a good way to receive free tokens, but they can also be riskier as they may result in the devaluation of the original cryptocurrency.

Airdrops from new projects: These airdrops are distributed by new blockchain projects as a way to gain exposure and build a community. Airdrops from new projects can be riskier as the project may not yet have a proven track record or established community.

By diversifying your portfolio with different types of airdrops, you can mitigate risk and increase your chances of receiving a significant return on your investment.

Here are some additional points on the topic of "Choosing Different Categories and Types of Airdrops":

ICO airdrops: Initial Coin Offerings (ICOs) are a popular way for new cryptocurrency projects to raise funds. Some ICOs may offer airdrops as a way to attract attention and generate interest in their project. Investors who participate in the ICO may receive free tokens, or they may be required to complete certain tasks to receive the airdrop.

Exchange airdrops: Some cryptocurrency exchanges may offer airdrops to users who hold a certain amount of a particular cryptocurrency on their exchange. This can be a way to incentivize users to trade and hold cryptocurrencies on their platform.

Fork airdrops: When a cryptocurrency undergoes a fork (a change to its underlying code), a new cryptocurrency may be created as a result. Some projects may distribute the new cryptocurrency to holders of the original cryptocurrency as an airdrop.

Staking airdrops

Some cryptocurrencies use a staking system, where users hold and lock up their tokens to help secure the network and receive rewards in return. Some projects may offer airdrops to users who stake their tokens.

Staking airdrops are a type of airdrop that rewards users for staking or holding a certain cryptocurrency. Staking is a process of holding a certain amount of cryptocurrency in a wallet or on a platform in order to support the network and earn rewards.

Staking airdrops can be a great way to earn passive income from your cryptocurrency holdings. The rewards are often paid out in the same cryptocurrency that is being staked, but can also be paid out in other tokens or even fiat currency.

However, it's important to note that staking often requires a certain level of technical expertise and understanding of the underlying blockchain technology. It also typically involves locking up your cryptocurrency for a certain period of time, which means you won't have immediate access to it.

Another consideration with staking airdrops is the potential for market volatility. The value of the cryptocurrency being staked can fluctuate, which can impact the overall value of the rewards earned through staking.

Overall, staking airdrops can be a valuable tool for earning passive income from your cryptocurrency holdings, but it's important to do your research and understand the risks and rewards before getting involved.

Staking airdrops are a type of airdrop that rewards users for staking or holding a particular cryptocurrency. Staking is the process of locking up or holding a certain amount of cryptocurrency in a wallet or on a platform to participate in the network's consensus mechanism and earn rewards.

With staking airdrops, users can receive additional tokens or rewards for staking their tokens for a certain period of time. The amount of tokens or rewards received can vary depending on the specific project and the length of time the tokens are staked.

Staking airdrops can be a great way to earn passive income from cryptocurrency holdings, as well as a way to support and participate in the growth of a particular network. However, it's important to note that staking comes with risks, such as the possibility of losing some or all of the staked tokens if the network experiences technical issues or other problems. Therefore, it's crucial to thoroughly research the project before staking and to only invest what you can afford to lose.

Community airdrops: Some cryptocurrency projects may offer airdrops to their existing community members as a way to reward and incentivize engagement. This can include tasks such as participating in social media, joining their telegram group, or referring new users to the project.

Airdrops for charity: Some cryptocurrency projects may offer airdrops as a way to support charitable causes or social initiatives. These airdrops may require participants to make a donation or contribute to a specific cause in order to receive the airdrop.

It's important to note that each type of airdrop comes with its own risks and benefits, and it's important to thoroughly research and evaluate each opportunity before investing. Additionally, it's important to ensure that the airdrop aligns with your investment goals and overall portfolio strategy.

Here are some more points to expand on the topic of "Choosing Different Categories and Types of Airdrops":

Utility vs. security tokens: Airdrops can be categorized into utility tokens, which are used to access a specific product or service, and security tokens, which represent an ownership stake in a company or asset. It's important to understand the difference between these two types of tokens, as they have different risks and potential returns.

Established vs. new projects: Some airdrops are offered by established projects with a track record of success, while others are offered by new and untested projects.

Investing in airdrops from established projects can provide more security and potentially lower risk, while investing in airdrops from new projects can offer higher potential returns but also higher risk.

Niche vs. mainstream projects

Airdrops can also be categorized based on the niche or mainstream appeal of the project. Niche projects may have a smaller user base but can offer unique and valuable services, while mainstream projects may have a larger user base but face more competition.

Niche vs. mainstream projects refer to the type of projects that are being offered in an airdrop. Niche projects are often focused on specific areas, such as blockchain-based gaming, supply chain management, or social media platforms. These projects may not have as much mainstream appeal, but they can offer unique and valuable services to users.

On the other hand, mainstream projects are often larger and more well-known, with a larger user base and wider appeal. These projects may offer more established services, such as payment processing or online marketplaces, but they may also face more competition from other established companies.

When it comes to airdrop investing, it's important to consider both niche and mainstream projects. Niche projects can offer unique opportunities for profit, as they may have less competition and offer specialized services that are in high demand.

However, mainstream projects may also present valuable opportunities, as they may have a larger user base and more established reputation.

Ultimately, the decision of whether to invest in a niche or mainstream project will depend on a number of factors, including the potential for profit, the level of competition, and the overall market conditions. It's important to do thorough research and analysis before making any investment decisions.

When it comes to airdrops, it's important to consider the niche or mainstream appeal of the project before investing. Niche projects may have a smaller user base but can offer unique and valuable services.

These projects may have a higher potential for growth and profitability if they can establish a loyal user base. However, they may also face challenges in gaining traction and attracting new users.

Mainstream projects, on the other hand, may have a larger user base and more established brand recognition. However, they also face more competition from other projects in the same space.

This can make it more difficult to stand out and attract new users, but it also means that there may be more opportunities for partnerships and collaborations with other established projects.

When considering niche vs. mainstream projects, it's important to look at factors such as the project's technology, team, and community.

Additionally, you should consider the potential for adoption and growth, as well as the competition in the market.

Ultimately, the best approach is to have a diversified portfolio that includes a mix of both niche and mainstream projects. This can help to mitigate risk and maximize potential returns.

Timeframe

Airdrops can also be categorized based on the timeframe of the investment. Some airdrops offer immediate rewards, while others require a longer-term investment strategy. It's important to consider your investment goals and timeline when choosing different types of airdrops.

When considering the timeframe of an airdrop investment, it's important to evaluate the potential risks and rewards associated with the investment.

Immediate reward airdrops, also known as "snapshots," typically require a short-term investment in order to receive the airdropped tokens. These airdrops can be attractive for traders looking for quick gains, but they also carry higher risks as the value of the tokens may not be sustained over time.

On the other hand, longer-term airdrops may require a more substantial investment of time and resources, but can potentially offer greater rewards.

For example, some airdrops may require participants to hold their tokens for a certain period of time in order to receive additional rewards or benefits.

It's important to carefully evaluate the timeframe of an airdrop investment and consider your own investment goals and risk tolerance before making any decisions.

Some investors may prefer a short-term approach for immediate gains, while others may be willing to take a longer-term view for potentially greater rewards.

Here are some additional details on the topic of Timeframe and airdrops:

Airdrops can have varying timeframes for reward distribution, which can affect the overall investment strategy. Some airdrops offer immediate rewards upon completion of specific tasks, such as following a project on social media or joining a telegram group.

These airdrops may be attractive for short-term investors looking for quick profits, but they may also be more volatile and risky.

Other airdrops may require a longer-term investment strategy, such as staking or holding tokens for a specific period of time before rewards are distributed.

These types of airdrops may be more attractive for investors looking to hold onto their assets for a longer period of time and take advantage of potential price appreciation.

It's important to carefully consider the timeframe of an airdrop and your investment goals before deciding to participate. Additionally, it's important to do your research and understand the requirements and potential risks associated with each airdrop before investing.

Geographical location: Some airdrops may only be available to investors in certain geographical locations, such as specific countries or regions.

It's important to check the eligibility requirements before investing in an airdrop to ensure that you are eligible to participate.

Overall, choosing different categories and types of airdrops can help you build a diversified portfolio that can mitigate risk and potentially provide higher returns.

It's important to consider various factors when choosing different types of airdrops, including the type of token, the project's track record, the timeframe of the investment, and any eligibility requirements.

Balancing Your Exposure and Allocations

When investing in airdrops, it's important to balance your exposure and allocations to reduce risk and maximize potential returns. One thing many people may not consider is the importance of rebalancing your portfolio regularly.

Rebalancing involves adjusting your portfolio allocations based on changes in the market or in your own investment goals. For example, if you initially allocated a large portion of your portfolio to a specific category of airdrops, but later discover that another category is showing more promise, you may want to rebalance your portfolio by reducing your exposure to the first category and increasing your exposure to the second.

Another important consideration is diversifying your exposure within each category of airdrops. For example, if you're investing in airdrops from different blockchain platforms, it's important to diversify within each platform by investing in different projects and tokens. This can help reduce the impact of any single project's success or failure on your overall portfolio.

It's also important to consider your risk tolerance when balancing your exposure and allocations. Some people may be comfortable with a higher risk, higher reward strategy that involves investing a larger portion of their portfolio in higher risk/higher reward airdrops. Others may prefer a more conservative approach that involves investing in lower risk, more established projects.

Ultimately, finding the right balance of exposure and allocation is a personal decision that depends on your investment goals, risk tolerance, and market conditions. Regularly reviewing and adjusting your portfolio can help you stay on track and maximize your investment potential.

When balancing exposure and allocations, it's important to consider various factors such as the risk level of the project, its potential for growth, and the current market conditions.

Many people overlook the importance of diversifying their portfolio and end up investing too heavily in one project, which can lead to significant losses if the project fails or experiences a sharp decline in value.

One strategy for balancing exposure is to allocate a certain percentage of your portfolio to high-risk/high-reward airdrops, while also investing in more established projects with a lower risk profile. It's also important to regularly review and rebalance your portfolio to ensure that you're maintaining a balanced exposure to different projects.

Another important factor to consider is the liquidity of the tokens you're investing in. Some airdrops may distribute tokens that have limited trading volume or are only available on less well-known exchanges.

This can make it difficult to sell your tokens or access your investment when you need to. It's important to research the liquidity of the tokens before investing and to consider investing in projects that have established trading markets on reputable exchanges.

Overall, balancing exposure and allocations is key to managing risk and maximizing the potential for returns in airdrop investing. It requires a thoughtful and strategic approach, as well as regular review and adjustment based on market conditions and project developments.

Rebalancing and Adjusting Your Strategy Over Time

When it comes to investing in airdrops or any other type of investment, it's important to regularly assess and adjust your investment strategy over time. This is where rebalancing comes in.

Rebalancing involves adjusting the proportions of assets in your portfolio to maintain a desired level of risk and return. This can help you avoid being over-exposed to any one asset or market, and can help ensure that your portfolio remains aligned with your investment goals.

One common rebalancing strategy is to periodically assess the performance of your portfolio and adjust your holdings accordingly. For example, if one asset class has performed well and increased in value, you may consider selling some of that asset and reallocating those funds to other areas of your portfolio that may have underperformed.

Another approach to rebalancing is to set a specific target allocation for each asset class in your portfolio and periodically adjust your holdings to maintain that allocation.

For example, you may decide to allocate 40% of your portfolio to airdrops, 30% to stocks, and 30% to bonds. If the value of your airdrops increases significantly, you may need to sell some of those assets and redistribute the funds to the other asset classes to maintain the desired allocation.

It's important to note that rebalancing can involve transaction fees and taxes, so it's important to consider these costs when deciding whether to rebalance your portfolio.

Overall, regularly assessing and adjusting your investment strategy through rebalancing can help you manage risk and maintain a diversified portfolio that aligns with your investment goals.

One important aspect of rebalancing and adjusting your airdrop investment strategy over time is staying up-to-date with the latest developments in the cryptocurrency market. This includes tracking the performance of your airdrops, monitoring the market trends and news, and evaluating the performance of your overall investment portfolio.

It is important to regularly assess whether your current strategy aligns with your investment goals and risk tolerance. As your investment portfolio grows and the market evolves, your goals and priorities may change.

This means that you may need to adjust your strategy to reflect these changes and to ensure that you are maximizing your returns while minimizing your risks.

Rebalancing can also help to address any imbalances in your portfolio, ensuring that you are not overly exposed to any one particular cryptocurrency or investment category. This can help to mitigate risks and protect your portfolio from any sudden price fluctuations or market volatility.

Another important consideration when rebalancing your portfolio is tax implications. Selling and buying assets can have tax implications, so it is important to consult with a tax professional or financial advisor to ensure that your rebalancing strategy is tax-efficient.

Overall, regularly assessing and adjusting your airdrop investment strategy can help to ensure that you are making the most of this investment opportunity and achieving your investment goals over time.

CHAPTER 5
MANAGING RISK AND AVOIDING SCAMS: STAYING SAFE AND SECURE

When it comes to investing in airdrops, managing risk and avoiding scams is crucial to ensure the safety and security of your investments. Here are some tips on how to stay safe:

Do your due diligence: Before investing in any airdrop, do your research and make sure to read the whitepaper and the project's website to understand their goals, roadmap, and team members. Look for credible sources of information to avoid scams and fraudulent projects.

Use reputable wallets and exchanges: Use trusted wallets and exchanges to store and trade your cryptocurrencies. Make sure to enable two-factor authentication (2FA) to secure your accounts.

Beware of phishing scams: Scammers often use phishing emails, social media, and messaging apps to trick users into giving away their private keys or passwords. Always double-check the sender's email address and do not click on suspicious links.

Avoid Ponzi schemes and MLMs: Be wary of airdrops that require you to recruit other users to earn rewards or promise unrealistic returns. These are often Ponzi schemes or multi-level marketing (MLM) scams.

Use discretion when sharing personal information: Be cautious when sharing personal information with airdrop projects, especially if they request sensitive data like your private keys or wallet addresses. Never share your private keys with anyone.

Don't fall for fake airdrops: Scammers often create fake airdrops that mimic legitimate projects to trick users into giving away their cryptocurrencies. Always verify the authenticity of an airdrop before investing in it.

By following these tips, you can minimize the risk of losing your investments to scams and fraudulent projects. Stay vigilant, keep learning, and always prioritize the safety and security of your investments.

One important aspect of managing risk when investing in airdrops is to avoid scams. Unfortunately, there are many fraudulent airdrops that are designed to trick investors into giving away their private keys or other sensitive information.

One common scam is the phishing scam, where a fake airdrop is set up to look like a legitimate one, but actually steals the investor's cryptocurrency. To avoid these scams, it's important to do your research and make sure that the airdrop is legitimate before investing.

Another way to manage risk is to diversify your portfolio across different types of airdrops and different cryptocurrency projects. This can help reduce your exposure to any single project or market, and increase your chances of success over the long term.

It's also important to keep your private keys and other sensitive information secure. This means using strong passwords and two-factor authentication, and avoiding public Wi-Fi networks when accessing your cryptocurrency wallets.

Additionally, you should always be wary of unsolicited messages or offers, and never give out your private keys or other sensitive information to anyone.

It's important to stay up-to-date with the latest developments in the cryptocurrency market, and be prepared to adjust your strategy as needed.

This means monitoring your portfolio regularly, and making changes as necessary to ensure that your investments are aligned with your goals and risk tolerance.

Identifying Red Flags and Warning Signs

When investing in airdrops, it's important to be aware of potential red flags and warning signs that may indicate a scam or fraudulent activity. Here are some things to keep in mind:

Lack of information: If a project has little to no information available, or if the information provided seems vague or incomplete, it may be a red flag. A legitimate project will usually have a detailed whitepaper, roadmap, and team information available for review.

Unrealistic promises: Be wary of projects that promise unrealistic returns or have overly ambitious goals without a clear plan to achieve them. Remember that there are no guarantees in the world of investing, and anything that seems too good to be true probably is.

Poor community engagement: A legitimate project will typically have an active and engaged community, with regular updates and communication from the team. If a project has little to no community engagement or communication, it may be a sign that the project is not legitimate.

Unprofessional website and branding: While a professional-looking website and branding do not guarantee the legitimacy of a project, a poorly designed or amateurish website and branding may be a warning sign.

Lack of transparency: Legitimate projects will usually be transparent about their funding, use of funds, and token distribution. If a project is not transparent about these details, it may be a red flag.

No clear use case: A legitimate project will typically have a clear use case or problem that it aims to solve. If a project has no clear use case or seems to be a copycat of another project without any added value, it may be a warning sign.

Suspicious team members: It's important to research the team members behind a project to ensure that they are legitimate and have a proven track record. If a team member has a history of fraudulent activity or has no visible online presence, it may be a red flag.

By being aware of these potential red flags and warning signs, investors can protect themselves from scams and fraudulent activity in the world of airdrop investing.

When it comes to identifying red flags and warning signs in the world of airdrops, it is important to be aware of the various tactics and strategies that scammers use to deceive investors.

Some of these tactics may not be immediately apparent, so it is important to be vigilant and conduct thorough research before investing in any airdrop.

One red flag to look out for is the lack of information about the project or team. If there is little to no information available about the project, its team members, or its advisors, this could be a warning sign that the project may not be legitimate. It is important to conduct extensive research and verify the credentials of the team members before investing in any airdrop.

Another red flag to be aware of is unrealistic promises or guarantees of returns. If an airdrop is promising unusually high returns with little to no effort, this could be a sign of a scam.

It is important to remember that no investment comes with a guarantee of returns, and if something seems too good to be true, it likely is.

Additionally, it is important to be wary of airdrops that require a significant upfront investment or ask for personal information such as passwords or private keys. Legitimate airdrops typically do not require any financial investment, and should not require any sensitive personal information.

Lastly, be cautious of airdrops that have poor or unprofessional website design, lack social media presence, or have questionable communication practices. These can be signs that the project is not being run by a professional team and could potentially be a scam.

In order to stay safe and secure when investing in airdrops, it is important to conduct thorough research, stay informed about the latest scams and warning signs, and remain vigilant for any red flags that may indicate a potential scam.

By taking the necessary precautions and avoiding scams, investors can maximize their potential returns and build a diversified portfolio of successful airdrop investments.

Protecting Your Private Keys and Passwords

Protecting your private keys and passwords is crucial when it comes to cryptocurrency investing, as they grant access to your funds and assets. Here are some lesser-known tips for protecting your private keys and passwords:

Use a Hardware Wallet: A hardware wallet is a physical device that stores your private keys offline, making them less vulnerable to hacking or theft.

These devices are considered the most secure way to store your cryptocurrency.

Enable Two-Factor Authentication: Two-factor authentication (2FA) adds an extra layer of security to your accounts by requiring a second verification step, such as a text message or authentication app. This can help prevent unauthorized access to your accounts.

Use Strong Passwords: Avoid using easily guessable passwords and instead opt for a combination of upper and lowercase letters, numbers, and symbols. You can use a password manager to generate and store complex passwords.

Be Mindful of Phishing Scams: Phishing scams are a common tactic used by hackers to gain access to your private keys and passwords. Be cautious of unsolicited emails or messages asking for your private information, and always verify the authenticity of the sender before sharing any information.

Backup Your Private Keys: It's important to backup your private keys in case your hardware wallet is lost or damaged. You can store a backup on a USB drive or other secure location, and ensure that it's encrypted and password-protected.

By following these tips, you can better protect your private keys and passwords and minimize the risk of losing your cryptocurrency investments to hacking or theft.

Here are some additional points to consider when it comes to protecting your private keys and passwords:

Use a strong and unique password: A strong password should be at least 12 characters long and include a mix of uppercase and lowercase letters, numbers, and symbols. Avoid using easily guessable information such as your name, birthdate, or common words.

Use two-factor authentication (2FA): 2FA adds an additional layer of security by requiring a second form of authentication, such as a text message or authentication app, in addition to your password.

Keep your private keys offline: Consider storing your private keys on an offline hardware wallet, such as a Trezor or Ledger Nano S. This helps protect your keys from being compromised by malware or hackers.

Back up your keys: Always keep a backup of your private keys in a safe and secure location. This ensures that you can still access your funds in case your device is lost or stolen.

Be cautious of phishing scams: Scammers may try to trick you into revealing your private keys or passwords through phishing scams, which can be difficult to detect. Always double-check the URL and website before entering any sensitive information.

Use a reputable wallet provider: When choosing a wallet provider, do your research and opt for a reputable and trusted company. Read reviews and check for any past security breaches or issues.

Regularly update your software: Keep your wallet software and any associated apps up to date to ensure that you have the latest security features and protections.

Learning from Past Mistakes and Lessons

When it comes to investing in airdrops, it's important to learn from past mistakes and lessons. Here are some things that many people may not know:

Learning from other people's experiences: There are many online forums and groups where investors share their experiences with different airdrops. Reading about other people's experiences can help you avoid making the same mistakes and identify potential warning signs.

Keeping track of your investments: Keeping a detailed record of your airdrop investments can help you identify trends and patterns over time. This can help you adjust your strategy and avoid making the same mistakes twice.

Staying up-to-date with the latest news and developments: The cryptocurrency market is constantly changing and evolving, so it's important to stay informed about the latest news and developments. This can help you identify potential risks and opportunities before they become widely known.

Understanding the impact of market conditions: The cryptocurrency market can be volatile and unpredictable, so it's important to understand how market conditions can impact your investments. This includes factors like market trends, regulatory changes, and global economic conditions.

Being patient and disciplined: Investing in airdrops can be a long-term strategy, and it's important to be patient and disciplined with your investments. Avoid making impulsive decisions and stick to your investment plan, even during times of market volatility.

By learning from past mistakes and lessons, investors can improve their strategies and increase their chances of success in the cryptocurrency market.

One thing many people may not know about learning from past mistakes and lessons is that it's not just about avoiding the same mistakes in the future. It's also about understanding the root causes of those mistakes and identifying any patterns or tendencies that may have led to them.

This can involve taking a closer look at your own decision-making process, emotions, and biases, and being honest with yourself about where you may have gone wrong.

Additionally, it's important to recognize that mistakes and failures are a natural part of any learning process, including airdrop investing. It's not uncommon for even experienced investors to make mistakes or experience losses, and it's important to approach these setbacks as opportunities for growth and learning.

Another aspect of learning from past mistakes is staying up-to-date with the latest developments in the cryptocurrency market and the airdrop landscape.

This can involve following reputable news sources, participating in online communities and forums, and attending industry events and conferences.

By staying informed and keeping an open mind, you can continue to refine your investment strategy and make more informed decisions in the future.

One important lesson to learn from the past is the importance of doing thorough research before investing in any cryptocurrency project or airdrop.

This includes not only reading the whitepaper and evaluating the team, but also investigating any past controversies or red flags associated with the project.

Another lesson is to be aware of market cycles and volatility. The cryptocurrency market has experienced significant highs and lows over the years, and it is important to be prepared for the possibility of market crashes or corrections.

This includes setting realistic expectations for returns and being prepared to hold onto investments for the long term.

Additionally, it is important to stay up-to-date with changes in regulations and legal frameworks surrounding cryptocurrency. Many countries are still developing their regulatory frameworks for cryptocurrencies, and it is important to be aware of any changes that may impact your investments.

Finally, it is important to be cautious of scams and fraudulent schemes. Many scams and fraudulent airdrops have been perpetrated in the past, and it is important to be able to identify warning signs and take steps to protect your investments and personal information.

CHAPTER *6*

ADVANCED STRATEGIES AND TOOLS: MAXIMIZING YOUR RETURNS

When it comes to advanced strategies and tools for maximizing returns on airdrop investments, there are several things that many people may not be aware of.

Here are a few examples:

Staking: Many blockchain projects offer a staking mechanism, which involves locking up your tokens for a period of time in exchange for rewards. By staking your tokens, you can earn additional tokens as a form of passive income, which can significantly boost your overall returns.

Yield farming

Yield farming involves lending your tokens to a decentralized finance (DeFi) platform in exchange for rewards. These rewards are often paid out in the platform's native token or in other tokens, and can be significantly higher than traditional interest rates.

Yield farming is a relatively new concept in the world of decentralized finance, and it has quickly gained popularity among crypto investors looking to maximize their returns. The basic idea behind yield farming is to lend your tokens to a DeFi platform in exchange for rewards, which are paid out in the platform's native token or other tokens.

Yield farming is often used in conjunction with liquidity provision, which involves adding liquidity to a decentralized exchange (DEX) by providing pairs of tokens in a pool. By doing this, liquidity providers earn a portion of the trading fees generated by the DEX. Yield farming takes this one step further by allowing liquidity providers to earn additional rewards in the form of tokens from the DeFi platform itself.

One of the key benefits of yield farming is the potential for high returns. Many DeFi platforms offer yields that are significantly higher than traditional interest rates, and some platforms offer yields of over 100% per year. However, it is important to note that these high returns often come with a high level of risk, as the DeFi space is still largely unregulated and subject to market volatility.

To participate in yield farming, investors must first choose a DeFi platform to lend their tokens to. This requires careful research and analysis to ensure that the platform is legitimate and has a strong track record of delivering on its promises. Once a platform has been chosen, investors must then transfer their tokens to the platform and begin lending them out. The rewards earned through yield farming can then be reinvested or traded on other platforms, further increasing the potential for returns.

As with any investment strategy, it is important to carefully consider the risks and benefits of yield farming before getting started. While the potential for high returns is certainly appealing, investors must be prepared to weather market volatility and potential losses. Additionally, it is important to stay up-to-date on the latest developments in the DeFi space, as the landscape is constantly evolving and new risks and opportunities may emerge over time.

Some additional information about yield farming:

Risks: Yield farming can be a high-risk strategy, as it involves lending your tokens to a DeFi platform that may not have a long track record or may be vulnerable to smart contract bugs or other security issues. Additionally, the rewards offered may fluctuate based on market conditions, so there is no guarantee of a steady return.

Impermanent loss: Yield farming on platforms that involve liquidity provision can also result in a phenomenon known as impermanent loss. This occurs when the price of one of the tokens in the pool changes significantly, causing the value of the tokens in the pool to diverge from the value of the tokens held by the yield farmer. As a result, the yield farmer may end up with fewer tokens overall than they initially deposited.

Strategies: Yield farming can be approached in a number of ways, including through liquidity provision on automated market maker platforms, staking tokens on DeFi protocols, or participating in yield farming pools that offer rewards for lending tokens. Advanced strategies such as leverage and hedging can also be employed to maximize returns.

Tools: There are a number of tools available to help yield farmers identify the best opportunities for maximizing their returns, including analytics platforms that track yield farming metrics such as APR, TVL, and impermanent loss, as well as bots and automated systems that can execute trades and move funds between yield farming pools. However, it is important to exercise caution when using these tools, as they can also introduce additional risks and may not always accurately reflect market conditions.

One thing to keep in mind when engaging in yield farming is the risk of impermanent loss. Impermanent loss is a temporary loss of funds that occurs when providing liquidity to a trading pair in an automated market maker (AMM) platform. This happens when the price of the two tokens in the trading pair diverges from the original price at which the liquidity was provided.

For example, if you provide liquidity to a trading pair with token A and token B at a 1:1 ratio and the price of token A increases, you will end up with a larger proportion of token A and a smaller proportion of token B in your pool. If you were to withdraw your liquidity at this point, you would end up with fewer total tokens than if you had simply held onto them.

To mitigate the risk of impermanent loss, some yield farming strategies involve only providing liquidity to stablecoin pairs or pairs with tokens that have a relatively stable price. Additionally, some yield farming platforms offer impermanent loss protection to users to compensate for any temporary losses incurred during liquidity provision.

It's important to thoroughly research and understand the risks involved in yield farming before getting started, as it can be a complex and volatile market.

Here are some additional points on yield farming:

Yield farming can be a complex and risky strategy, as it involves understanding the nuances of different DeFi platforms and their respective rewards systems. It's important to thoroughly research and understand the risks before investing.

Some yield farming platforms may have limited liquidity or be subject to liquidity issues, which can affect the value of rewards and make it difficult to withdraw funds. This is something to consider when choosing a platform to participate in.

Yield farming also typically requires a significant investment of time and effort to monitor and adjust your investments, as rewards and returns can fluctuate rapidly. This may not be a feasible strategy for everyone.

Some yield farming platforms may have high transaction fees, which can eat into the profits from rewards. It's important to factor in these fees when calculating potential returns.

Yield farming can also have tax implications, as rewards may be considered taxable income. It's important to consult with a tax professional to understand the tax implications of yield farming.

It's worth noting that yield farming is a relatively new and rapidly evolving space in the cryptocurrency world. It's important to stay up-to-date on the latest developments and trends, as the landscape can change quickly.

Arbitrage

Arbitrage involves taking advantage of price discrepancies between different exchanges or markets to make a profit. While this strategy can be risky, it can also be highly profitable if done correctly.

Arbitrage is a trading strategy that seeks to profit from differences in price between different markets or exchanges. In the context of cryptocurrency, this can involve buying a cryptocurrency on one exchange where it is undervalued and immediately selling it on another exchange where it is overvalued, in order to make a profit on the price difference.

Arbitrage can be a highly profitable strategy, but it can also be risky. The key to successful arbitrage is to move quickly and efficiently to take advantage of price discrepancies before they disappear. This requires careful monitoring of multiple exchanges and markets, as well as a solid understanding of market trends and price movements.

In addition to traditional exchange-based arbitrage, there are also opportunities for triangular arbitrage, which involves taking advantage of price discrepancies between three different cryptocurrencies. This strategy can be even more complex than traditional arbitrage, but can also offer higher potential returns.

It's important to note that arbitrage opportunities in the cryptocurrency market can be fleeting and highly competitive, and there is always the risk of sudden price fluctuations or market volatility. As with any trading strategy, it's important to conduct thorough research and analysis before engaging in arbitrage, and to never invest more than you can afford to lose.

Arbitrage in cryptocurrency refers to the practice of buying and selling the same digital asset across different exchanges or markets simultaneously to profit from price discrepancies. The goal of arbitrage is to buy the asset on one exchange where the price is lower and sell it on another exchange where the price is higher.

For example, if Bitcoin is trading at $50,000 on Exchange A and $50,500 on Exchange B, a trader can buy Bitcoin on Exchange A and immediately sell it on Exchange B for a profit of $500. This is because the trader can buy Bitcoin for a lower price on Exchange A and then sell it for a higher price on Exchange B.

However, arbitrage opportunities are often short-lived, as they tend to disappear quickly as traders exploit the price difference. This means that traders need to act quickly to take advantage of arbitrage opportunities before they disappear.

Arbitrage can be risky as it requires a significant amount of capital to make a profit, and there is always the risk of price volatility and exchange hacks. Additionally, some exchanges may charge fees or have limits on the amount of cryptocurrency that can be withdrawn, which can affect the profitability of the strategy.

It's important to note that arbitrage is not suitable for all traders and should be approached with caution. Traders should thoroughly research and understand the risks and potential rewards before engaging in arbitrage trading.

Trading bots: Trading bots are automated software programs that can execute trades on your behalf based on predefined criteria. These bots can be programmed to take advantage of market trends and patterns, and can help you maximize your returns while minimizing your risk.

Airdrop aggregators

Airdrop aggregators are platforms that help you discover and participate in multiple airdrops at once. These platforms can save you time and effort by providing a centralized location for all of your airdrop investments.

Airdrop aggregators are websites or platforms that collect and list airdrops from different projects in one place. These aggregators provide users with an easy and convenient way to keep track of upcoming airdrops, as well as a way to discover new projects and tokens.

One benefit of using an airdrop aggregator is that it saves time and effort that would otherwise be spent searching for airdrops across different platforms and social media channels.

Aggregators also often provide additional information and insights about the airdrops, such as the project's whitepaper, team members, and token economics.

However, it's important to be cautious when using airdrop aggregators, as not all listed airdrops may be legitimate. Some aggregators may list airdrops from scam projects or projects with questionable backgrounds, which could result in users losing their funds or personal information.

Therefore, it's important to do thorough research and exercise caution before participating in any airdrops listed on an aggregator.

Airdrop aggregators are websites or platforms that collect and curate airdrop campaigns from different projects and display them in one place. These aggregators can be a convenient way for investors to discover and participate in airdrops without having to search for them individually.

Some airdrop aggregators may also offer additional features, such as airdrop alerts, customized portfolios, and analytics tools to help investors track their airdrop earnings. However, it's important to note that not all airdrop aggregators are reliable, and some may promote fraudulent or scam airdrops.

Investors should always do their own research and due diligence before participating in any airdrop campaign, regardless of whether they discovered it through an aggregator or not.

Additionally, it's important to maintain proper security measures when participating in airdrops, such as using a separate wallet address and never sharing private keys or passwords.

Overall, these advanced strategies and tools require more knowledge, experience, and technical expertise than basic airdrop investing. However, if done correctly, they can help you maximize your returns and achieve your investment goals.

One advanced strategy for maximizing returns in airdrop investing is using airdrop aggregators. Airdrop aggregators are websites or platforms that collect information about upcoming and ongoing airdrops, making it easier for investors to keep track of potential opportunities. These platforms can also provide tools for tracking airdrop rewards and managing portfolios.

Another advanced tool is using cryptocurrency trading bots to automate the buying and selling of cryptocurrencies. Trading bots can be programmed to execute trades based on a set of predefined criteria, such as market trends or price movements, and can operate 24/7 without the need for constant monitoring. However, it's important to note that trading bots come with their own risks, such as technical glitches and hacking vulnerabilities.

Some investors also employ margin trading, which involves borrowing funds to increase the amount of cryptocurrency they can purchase. This strategy can magnify returns but also comes with increased risks, as losses can exceed the initial investment.

It's important for advanced investors to stay up-to-date with the latest developments in the cryptocurrency market and adapt their strategies accordingly. This may involve keeping track of industry news and trends, networking with other investors and experts, and continually evaluating and adjusting investment portfolios.

Here are some additional advanced strategies and tools that can help investors maximize their returns in airdrop investing:

Trading bots: Some investors use trading bots to automatically execute trades based on specific market conditions or indicators. These bots can help traders take advantage of opportunities quickly and efficiently.

Technical analysis

Technical analysis involves analyzing charts and market data to identify patterns and trends that can help predict future price movements. This strategy can be useful for investors who want to time their trades more effectively.

Technical analysis is a method of evaluating securities and predicting their future price movements by analyzing statistics generated by market activity, such as price and volume. Here are some things that many people may not know about technical analysis:

It is based on the idea that market trends, patterns, and cycles repeat themselves over time, and that these patterns can be identified and used to make trading decisions.

Technical analysts use various tools and techniques to analyze market data, including chart patterns, trend lines, moving averages, and technical indicators such as the Relative Strength Index (RSI) and the Moving Average Convergence Divergence (MACD).

Technical analysis is not an exact science and can be subjective. Two analysts looking at the same chart may come up with different interpretations and predictions.

Technical analysis is not a crystal ball and cannot predict the future with 100% accuracy. It is important to combine technical analysis with other forms of analysis and to have a comprehensive trading strategy.

Technical analysis can be applied to any financial market, including stocks, forex, commodities, and cryptocurrencies.

Technical analysis can be time-consuming and requires practice and experience to master. There are many resources available, such as books, courses, and online communities, to help traders learn and improve their technical analysis skills.

Technical analysis is a method of evaluating market trends, patterns, and price movements using statistical tools and charts.

It can be used to make predictions about future price movements based on past data. Some techniques used in technical analysis include chart patterns, moving averages, and trendlines.

One important thing to note about technical analysis is that it does not consider the fundamental factors affecting an asset's value, such as the company's financial performance or news events.

As such, it should be used in conjunction with fundamental analysis to gain a more comprehensive understanding of an asset's potential value.

Another important aspect of technical analysis is that it is based on the assumption that market trends and patterns are repeatable and predictable. However, this may not always be the case, as market conditions can change quickly and unpredictably.

Therefore, it's important to exercise caution and use technical analysis as one tool in a larger investment strategy.

Fundamental analysis

Fundamental analysis involves analyzing the underlying value of an asset based on factors such as the project's development roadmap, team, and partnerships. This strategy can be useful for investors who want to identify undervalued projects and hold them for the long term.

Fundamental analysis is a method of evaluating an asset's intrinsic value by examining its underlying economic and financial factors. This analysis includes studying macroeconomic indicators, such as interest rates, inflation, and unemployment, as well as microeconomic factors, such as company financial statements, industry trends, and competitive landscape.

What many people may not know is that fundamental analysis is often used in the stock market to evaluate individual stocks or the overall market. However, it can also be applied to other assets such as cryptocurrencies and commodities.

One key aspect of fundamental analysis is examining a company's financial statements, including its balance sheet, income statement, and cash flow statement. This allows investors to evaluate a company's financial health and performance, such as its revenue growth, profitability, and debt levels.

Another aspect of fundamental analysis is evaluating a company's competitive position within its industry. This includes analyzing the company's market share, product offerings, and pricing strategies, as well as examining the broader industry trends and competitive landscape.

In addition to analyzing individual companies, fundamental analysis can also be used to evaluate entire markets or economies. This includes examining macroeconomic indicators such as GDP growth, interest rates, and inflation, as well as geopolitical factors such as trade policies and political instability.

Overall, fundamental analysis is a powerful tool for investors and traders to evaluate the underlying value of an asset and make informed investment decisions. By analyzing both macro and microeconomic factors, investors can gain a deeper understanding of the asset's financial health, competitive position, and potential for future growth.

Here are some additional points to consider when it comes to fundamental analysis in the context of cryptocurrency:

Regulatory environment: Keep an eye on the regulatory environment surrounding cryptocurrencies. Government policies and regulations can significantly impact the value of a cryptocurrency. For instance, if a government announces that it will ban cryptocurrency trading, it can cause a sharp drop in the value of affected cryptocurrencies.

Community and development: The strength of a cryptocurrency's community and development team can play a significant role in its value.

Check the cryptocurrency's social media platforms, forums, and development updates to gauge the community's engagement and the development team's activity. Active communities and a dedicated development team can signal that the cryptocurrency has a strong foundation.

Adoption and partnerships: The adoption of cryptocurrencies by merchants and businesses can increase their value. Partnerships with established businesses can also bring credibility to the cryptocurrency and drive its adoption.

Look for cryptocurrencies that have strong partnerships and are being adopted by merchants, as this can signal a promising future for the asset.

Whitepapers: A cryptocurrency's whitepaper is a document that outlines the cryptocurrency's vision, goals, and technology. Reading a cryptocurrency's whitepaper can help you understand the technology behind the cryptocurrency and its potential for success.

Look for whitepapers that are well-written, provide detailed information, and have a clear roadmap for development.

Market capitalization: The market capitalization of a cryptocurrency is its total value in circulation. Market capitalization is an essential metric to consider when analyzing cryptocurrencies, as it can give you an idea of the cryptocurrency's overall value and popularity.

A cryptocurrency with a high market capitalization is more likely to have more liquidity and be more stable than one with a low market capitalization.

Token economics: Token economics refer to the rules that govern how a cryptocurrency functions, such as its supply and demand, and the incentives for using and holding the cryptocurrency.

Understanding the token economics of a cryptocurrency can help you evaluate its long-term value proposition.

Competition: Finally, consider the competition that a cryptocurrency faces from other cryptocurrencies in the market. A cryptocurrency that is competing against similar projects may struggle to gain traction and have a lower value proposition.

Conversely, a cryptocurrency that offers unique features and solves a problem that other cryptocurrencies do not may have a significant advantage over its competition.

Margin trading: Margin trading involves borrowing funds from a broker to trade with more capital than you have in your account. This strategy can be risky but can also lead to higher returns if used correctly.

Staking: Staking involves holding and locking up cryptocurrency in a network to help secure the blockchain and earn rewards. This strategy can be a source of passive income for investors who want to hold a cryptocurrency long-term.

Yield farming: Yield farming involves providing liquidity to decentralized finance (DeFi) protocols in exchange for rewards. This strategy can be a source of passive income for investors who are willing to take on some risk.

Overall, these advanced strategies and tools require more knowledge and experience than the basic strategies discussed earlier. It's important for investors to do their own research and due diligence before implementing any of these strategies.

Leveraging Staking, Yield Farming, and Liquidity Mining

Staking, yield farming, and liquidity mining are popular ways of earning rewards in the cryptocurrency world, but there are some important factors to consider before diving in.

First, staking involves holding a certain amount of a particular cryptocurrency in a designated wallet and participating in the network's consensus mechanism by validating transactions. In exchange for this service, stakers receive rewards in the form of additional coins or tokens. However, staking requires a significant amount of capital to be locked up for a certain period of time, which can limit liquidity and investment flexibility.

Yield farming, on the other hand, involves lending tokens to a DeFi platform and earning rewards in return. These rewards can be in the platform's native token or other tokens, and the interest rates can be significantly higher than traditional savings accounts. However, yield farming carries a higher level of risk due to the volatility and newness of the DeFi ecosystem. It is important to thoroughly research the platform and assess the risks before investing.

Liquidity mining is a form of yield farming that involves providing liquidity to a decentralized exchange (DEX) by depositing pairs of tokens.

In return, liquidity providers (LPs) receive a share of the transaction fees generated on the DEX. Similar to yield farming, liquidity mining carries a higher level of risk and requires thorough research and risk management.

It's important to note that staking, yield farming, and liquidity mining are not without risks, and investors should thoroughly research and assess the risks before investing. Additionally, investors should also consider the tax implications of earning rewards through these methods, as they may be subject to capital gains taxes.

Here are some additional details on leveraging staking, yield farming, and liquidity mining:

Staking: In addition to earning rewards through airdrops, staking is another way to earn passive income in the cryptocurrency world. Staking involves holding and locking up a certain amount of tokens as collateral to validate transactions on the blockchain network.

In exchange for this service, stakers are rewarded with more tokens. The more tokens a user stakes, the higher the potential rewards. However, staking comes with the risk of slashing, which is a penalty for dishonest behavior on the network.

Yield farming: Yield farming involves lending your tokens to a decentralized finance (DeFi) platform in exchange for rewards. These rewards are often paid out in the platform's native token or in other tokens, and can be significantly higher than traditional interest rates.

Yield farming requires users to actively manage their investments and move their tokens between different liquidity pools to maximize returns. It also comes with the risk of impermanent loss, which occurs when the value of one token in a liquidity pool changes relative to another token.

Liquidity mining: Liquidity mining is a specific type of yield farming that focuses on providing liquidity to decentralized exchanges (DEXs).

Users can provide liquidity to a DEX by depositing an equal value of two different tokens into a liquidity pool. In exchange, users receive tokens that represent their share of the liquidity pool.

These tokens can then be staked to earn rewards in the form of the DEX's native token. Liquidity mining requires careful consideration of the risks associated with providing liquidity, such as the potential for price slippage and impermanent loss.

Overall, staking, yield farming, and liquidity mining are all strategies that require careful consideration of the risks involved. It's important for investors to do their research and understand the potential rewards and downsides before committing their funds to any strategy.

One thing that many people may not know about leveraging staking, yield farming, and liquidity mining is that it can be risky and require a significant amount of effort and attention.

While the potential returns can be high, there is also a possibility of losing your investment, especially if you do not fully understand the mechanisms behind these strategies. Additionally, some DeFi platforms may be vulnerable to hacks or exploits, which can result in the loss of funds.

It is important to thoroughly research and understand the risks and potential rewards before participating in staking, yield farming, or liquidity mining. It is also important to diversify your portfolio and not invest more than you can afford to lose.

Keeping up to date with the latest developments and news in the DeFi space can also be helpful in identifying potential risks and opportunities.

Using Analytics, Trading Bots, and Signals

When it comes to investing in cryptocurrencies, there are several tools and strategies available that can help traders make informed decisions and maximize their returns. One of these strategies is using analytics, trading bots, and signals. Here are some things that many people may not know about using these tools:

Analytics

Cryptocurrency analytics platforms provide traders with valuable data insights, including market trends, price movements, and trading volumes. These platforms use various indicators and charting tools to help traders make more informed decisions. However, it's important to note that analytics platforms are not foolproof and should be used as part of a comprehensive trading strategy.

Cryptocurrency analytics platforms have become increasingly popular among traders as the crypto market continues to grow and evolve. These platforms provide traders with valuable insights into market trends and price movements that can be used to make more informed trading decisions.

Some of the key features of cryptocurrency analytics platforms include:

Charting tools: These platforms often offer advanced charting tools that allow traders to view price movements and analyze trends over different time frames. These tools can help traders identify patterns and make predictions about future price movements.

Indicators: Cryptocurrency analytics platforms also offer a range of technical indicators that can be used to analyze market trends and identify potential trading opportunities. These indicators include moving averages, RSI, MACD, and more.

Market data: These platforms also provide real-time market data, including trading volumes, order books, and price data. This information can be used to gauge market sentiment and identify potential buying or selling opportunities.

News and social media sentiment analysis: Some analytics platforms also provide news and social media sentiment analysis, which can be used to gauge market sentiment and identify potential market-moving events.

While cryptocurrency analytics platforms can be a valuable tool for traders, it's important to remember that they are not foolproof. Market conditions can change quickly, and no platform can predict the future with 100% accuracy.

Traders should always use analytics platforms as part of a comprehensive trading strategy that takes into account a range of factors, including market conditions, risk tolerance, and personal investment goals.

One important thing to note when using cryptocurrency analytics platforms is that not all platforms are created equal. Some platforms may be more reliable and accurate than others, and it's important to do your own research and due diligence to determine which platform best fits your needs.

Another important consideration is that analytics platforms are not a substitute for fundamental analysis and market research. While analytics can provide valuable insights, they should be used in conjunction with other tools and strategies to make well-informed trading decisions.

Additionally, some traders may choose to use trading bots and signals in conjunction with analytics platforms. Trading bots are software programs that can automatically execute trades based on predetermined rules and algorithms.

Signals, on the other hand, are notifications or alerts that indicate when a specific trade or action should be taken based on market conditions.

While these tools can be helpful, it's important to use caution and carefully consider the risks involved. Trading bots and signals can be vulnerable to hacking and other security issues, and they may not always be accurate or reliable.

As with any trading strategy, it's important to do your own research, assess the risks, and use these tools in a way that aligns with your overall investment goals and risk tolerance.

Here are some additional insights on the topic of cryptocurrency analytics:

Choosing the right analytics platform: There are numerous cryptocurrency analytics platforms available, each with its own set of features and tools. It's important to choose a platform that fits your trading style and preferences. Some popular options include CoinMarketCap, TradingView, CryptoCompare, and Coinigy.

Understanding the data: While analytics platforms provide valuable insights, it's crucial to understand the data being presented. This includes understanding the different types of charts and indicators, as well as the meaning behind certain metrics such as trading volume and market capitalization.

Combining multiple sources: It's often beneficial to combine data from multiple sources to gain a more comprehensive understanding of the market. This can include using multiple analytics platforms, as well as incorporating data from news sources, social media, and other sources.

Using backtesting: Backtesting is the process of testing a trading strategy using historical data. Many analytics platforms offer backtesting tools, which can be helpful for evaluating the effectiveness of different trading strategies.

Monitoring market sentiment: Cryptocurrency analytics platforms can also provide insights into market sentiment, including social media mentions and sentiment analysis. This can be useful for identifying potential market trends and making informed trading decisions.

Trading bots

Trading bots are automated programs that execute trades based on pre-set rules and parameters. They can be helpful in taking advantage of market fluctuations, but they require careful monitoring to ensure they are operating effectively. It's important to note that some trading bots may come with hidden fees, so be sure to read the terms and conditions carefully before using one.

In addition to the potential benefits of trading bots, there are also some limitations and risks to consider. One potential issue is that trading bots are only as good as the rules and parameters they are programmed with, which may not account for unexpected market events or changes in market conditions.

Another risk is that trading bots can be susceptible to hacks or security breaches, especially if they are not properly secured or maintained. It's important to choose a reputable trading bot provider and to use strong security measures, such as two-factor authentication and secure passwords.

Additionally, it's important to monitor the performance of your trading bot regularly and make adjustments as needed. This can include tweaking the rules and parameters or even turning the bot off entirely if it is not performing as expected.

Ultimately, trading bots can be a useful tool for experienced traders, but they should be used as part of a comprehensive trading strategy and with careful consideration of the potential risks and limitations.

Some trading bots use machine learning algorithms to improve their performance over time, while others rely on simple rule-based strategies. It's important to understand the underlying logic of the trading bot you are using, as well as its limitations.

One potential drawback of trading bots is that they can be vulnerable to sudden market movements that are not accounted for in their programming. For example, if a major news event causes a sudden price spike or drop, a trading bot may continue to execute trades based on its pre-set rules, leading to unexpected losses.

It's also important to be aware of the potential risks involved in using trading bots, such as technical glitches, hacking, and errors in the bot's programming. Some bots may also be designed to scam users, so it's important to do your due diligence before using any trading bot.

Overall, trading bots can be a useful tool for experienced traders who are able to carefully monitor their performance and adjust their strategies as needed. However, they should not be relied upon as a substitute for careful research and analysis.

Signals

Trading signals are alerts that inform traders of potential trading opportunities based on market analysis. Signals can be delivered through email, SMS, or directly through a trading platform. While signals can be helpful in identifying market trends, it's important to note that they should not be relied on solely for making trading decisions.

In addition to the information provided, it's important to note that trading signals can be generated in different ways. Some signals are generated by humans who analyze the market and make predictions based on their analysis. Other signals are generated by algorithms that use complex mathematical models and historical data to make predictions.

It's important to carefully evaluate the quality and reliability of the trading signals you use. Some signal providers may make exaggerated claims about their accuracy, and it's important to do your own research and verify their claims before relying on their signals.

Additionally, it's important to consider the timing of signals. Some signals may be generated based on short-term market fluctuations, while others may be based on longer-term trends. It's important to consider your own trading goals and strategies when evaluating signals to ensure they align with your overall approach.

It's important to remember that trading signals are just one tool in a trader's toolkit, and should be used in conjunction with other analysis and research. While signals can provide valuable insights into the market, they should not be relied on as the sole source of information when making trading decisions.

Choosing the right tools: With so many analytics platforms, trading bots, and signal providers available, it can be overwhelming to choose the right one. It's important to do your research and choose a reputable provider that offers the features you need.

Additionally, be aware that many of these tools come with a cost, so factor this into your overall trading strategy.

Understanding the risks: While using analytics, trading bots, and signals can be helpful in making informed trading decisions, they do not eliminate risk entirely.

It's important to understand the risks associated with investing in cryptocurrencies and to always practice proper risk management strategies. Additionally, be wary of any tools or strategies that promise guaranteed returns or unrealistic results.

Using analytics, trading bots, and signals can be a powerful tool for crypto traders, but there are some things that many people may not know.

First, while these tools can be helpful, they should not be relied upon entirely. It is important to use your own judgment and analysis in addition to the signals and data provided by these tools.

Second, there are many different types of trading bots and signal providers available, and not all of them are created equal. Some may be scams or provide inaccurate information, so it is important to do your research and choose a reputable provider.

Third, even if you are using a trading bot or signal provider, it is important to keep up to date with news and events that may impact the market. Sudden changes in regulations or security breaches can greatly impact the value of cryptocurrencies, and these events may not be reflected in the data provided by the tools.

It is important to use these tools responsibly and not become overly reliant on them. They can be a helpful tool for identifying trends and opportunities, but they should not be used to make all of your trading decisions.

It is still important to have a solid understanding of the market and to use your own judgment when making investment decisions.

Collaborating with Communities and Networks

Collaborating with communities and networks can be a powerful way to stay up-to-date with the latest trends and developments in the cryptocurrency space. Many cryptocurrency projects have active online communities where members can share ideas, ask questions, and discuss the latest news.

One thing that many people may not realize is that being an active member of a cryptocurrency community can also be a valuable networking opportunity.

By participating in online forums and social media groups, you can connect with other like-minded individuals who share your interests and goals. This can lead to valuable collaborations and partnerships that can help you achieve your objectives.

Another benefit of collaborating with communities and networks is that you can learn from the experiences of others. By sharing your own experiences and listening to the experiences of others, you can gain a deeper understanding of the cryptocurrency market and the opportunities and risks that it presents.

It's also worth noting that many cryptocurrency projects offer rewards and incentives for community members who contribute in meaningful ways. For example, some projects offer bounties for bug reports, while others offer rewards for participating in their governance process. By taking advantage of these incentives, you can earn cryptocurrency while also contributing to the success of the project.

Overall, collaborating with communities and networks can be a valuable way to stay informed, network with like-minded individuals, and contribute to the success of cryptocurrency projects.

Here are some additional points on collaborating with communities and networks in the context of cryptocurrency:

Community-driven projects: Many successful cryptocurrency projects have been driven by communities rather than large corporations. By working closely with a community of users, developers can gain valuable insights and feedback, leading to more effective and user-friendly products.

Moreover, community-driven projects often have a more decentralized structure, which can be beneficial in terms of transparency and avoiding single points of failure.

Participating in online forums: Online forums such as Reddit and Discord can be excellent resources for learning about new projects and collaborating with other cryptocurrency enthusiasts. By participating in these forums, individuals can gain valuable insights into market trends, potential investment opportunities, and emerging technologies.

Joining cryptocurrency communities: Joining a cryptocurrency community can provide a range of benefits, including access to exclusive information, networking opportunities, and early access to new projects.

For example, some cryptocurrency communities offer members early access to new coins or tokens as a reward for active participation.

Attending cryptocurrency events: Attending cryptocurrency events can be an effective way to network with other industry professionals and gain valuable insights into the latest trends and technologies. Many events also offer opportunities for collaboration and partnership building.

Supporting open-source projects: Many cryptocurrency projects are open-source, meaning that the code is freely available for anyone to use and modify.

By supporting these projects and contributing to their development, individuals can help build stronger and more collaborative communities.

Overall, collaborating with communities and networks can be an effective way to stay informed and engaged in the rapidly evolving cryptocurrency ecosystem.

By working together, individuals and organizations can help build a more transparent, decentralized, and innovative financial system.

Collaborating with communities and networks can be a powerful tool for cryptocurrency traders and investors. Many cryptocurrencies have strong communities built around them, and these communities often have a wealth of knowledge and information that can be useful for traders.

By collaborating with these communities and networks, traders can gain access to valuable insights and information about a particular cryptocurrency, including its development progress, upcoming events, and potential price movements.

Additionally, communities and networks can provide a platform for traders to connect and collaborate with like-minded individuals, share ideas and strategies, and support each other.

One thing many people may not know about collaborating with communities and networks is the importance of being an active and engaged member. It's not enough to simply join a community or network and expect to benefit from it.

Traders need to actively participate in discussions, share their knowledge and expertise, and build relationships with other members.

By doing so, they can establish themselves as valuable contributors to the community and gain access to even more valuable insights and information.

Chapter 7

CONCLUSION: AIRDROP INVESTING AS A SUSTAINABLE AND PROFITABLE VENTURE.

One thing that many people may not know is that airdrop investing can be a sustainable and profitable venture, but it requires patience, careful research, and a long-term approach. While it can be tempting to chase quick gains through airdrops and other speculative investments, it's important to remember that the crypto market is volatile and unpredictable.

To be successful in airdrop investing, it's important to have a well-rounded strategy that incorporates a variety of techniques, such as diversification, risk management, and advanced tools like yield farming and trading bots.

Additionally, it's crucial to stay informed and up-to-date on industry trends and developments, and to continually adjust and refine your strategy over time.

Finally, it's important to approach airdrop investing with a long-term mindset and a commitment to sustainability. This means investing in projects that align with your values and have a strong community and development team, rather than simply chasing short-term gains.

By following these principles, investors can maximize their returns while also contributing to the growth and sustainability of the crypto ecosystem as a whole.

One important aspect of airdrop investing that people may not know about is the potential long-term benefits of participating in early-stage projects. While the immediate rewards of airdrops may be enticing, the true value of these projects may not be fully realized until years down the line.

By investing in promising projects early on and building a relationship with their communities, investors may be able to benefit from future token appreciation and other rewards as the project grows and develops.

Another important consideration is the ethical implications of investing in certain projects. It's important to do your research and ensure that the projects you are investing in align with your personal values and beliefs.

Additionally, investors should be aware of the potential for scams and fraudulent projects in the airdrop space and take steps to protect themselves from these risks.

In conclusion, airdrop investing can be a sustainable and profitable venture for those who approach it with a comprehensive strategy and a willingness to learn and adapt.

By staying informed about market trends, leveraging advanced tools and strategies, and collaborating with communities and networks, investors can increase their chances of success in this exciting and dynamic space.

However, it's important to approach airdrop investing with caution and diligence, and always prioritize risk management and security.

www.ingramcontent.com/pod-product-compliance
Lightning Source LLC
Chambersburg PA
CBHW031534210526
45464CB00013B/766